Born in 1927

By

Kerry Butters.

Born in 1927

Millennium:	**2nd millennium**

Centuries:	19th century – **20th century** – 21st century

Decades:	1890s 1900s 1910s – **1920s** – 1930s 1940s 1950s

Years:	1924 1925 1926 – **1927** – 1928 1929 1930

1927 (MCMXXVII) was a common year starting on Saturday (dominical letter B) of the Gregorian calendar and a common year starting on Friday (dominical letter C) of the Julian calendar, the 1927th year of the Common Era (CE) and *Anno Domini* (AD) designations, the 927th year of the 2nd millennium, the 27th year of the 20th century, and the 8th year of the 1920s decade. Note that the Julian day for 1927 is 13 calendar days difference, which continued to be used from 1582 until the complete conversion of the Gregorian calendar was entirely done in 1929.

Contents

Events

January

- January 1 – The Cristero War erupts in Mexico when Catholic rebels attack the government, which had placed heavy restrictions on the Catholic Church.
- January 7 – The first transatlantic telephone call is made *via radio* from New York City to London.
- January 7 – The Harlem Globetrotters play their first ever road game in Hinckley, Illinois.
- January 9 – A military rebellion is crushed in Lisbon, Portugal.
- January 15 – Teddy Wakelam gives the first sports commentary on BBC Radio.
- January 19 – Great Britain sends troops to China to protect foreign nationals from spreading anti-foreign riots in Central China.
- January 24 – U.S. marines invade Nicaragua by orders of President Calvin Coolidge, intervening in the Nicaraguan Civil War and remaining in the country until 1933.
- January 30 – Right-wing veterans and the *Republikanischer Schutzbund* clash in Schattendorf, Austria, with two fatalities resulting (see also July 15).

February

- February – Werner Heisenberg formulates his famous uncertainty principle while employed as a lecturer at Niels Bohr's Institute for Theoretical Physics at the University of Copenhagen.

- February 12 – The first British troops land in Shanghai.
- February 14 – An earthquake in Yugoslavia kills 100.
- February 19
  - A general strike in Shanghai protests the presence of British troops.
  - In the United States, the silent romantic comedy film *It* starring Clara Bow, is released, popularising the concept of the "It girl".
- February 23 – The U.S. Federal Radio Commission (later renamed the Federal Communications Commission) begins to regulate the use of radio frequencies.

March

- March 4 – A diamond rush in South Africa includes trained athletes that have been hired by major companies to stake claims.
- March 7 – The 7.0 Mw Kita Tango earthquake kills at least 2,925 in the Toyooka and Mineyama areas, western Honshu, Japan.
- March 10 – Albania mobilizes in case of an attack by Yugoslavia.
- March 11
  - In New York City, the Roxy Theatre is opened by Samuel Roxy Rothafel.
  - The first armored car robbery is committed by the Flatheads Gang near Pittsburgh.
- March 13 – Fritz Lang's culturally influential film *Metropolis* premieres in Germany.
- March 24 – Nanking Incident: After six foreigners have been killed in Nanking and it appears that Kuomintang and Communist Party of China forces would overrun the foreign consulates, warships of the U.S. Navy and the British Royal Navy fire shells and shot to disperse the crowds.

April

- April 1 – The U.S. Bureau of Prohibition is founded (under the Department of the Treasury).
- April 5 – In Britain, the Trade Disputes and Trade Unions Act 1927 forbids strikes of support.
- April 7 – Bell Telephone Co. transmits an image of Herbert Hoover (then the Secretary of Commerce), which becomes the first successful long distance demonstration of television.
- April 12
  - The Royal and Parliamentary Titles Act 1927 renames the United Kingdom of Great Britain and Ireland as the United Kingdom of Great Britain and Northern Ireland. The change acknowledges that the Irish Free State is no longer part of the Kingdom.
  - Kuomintang troops kill a number of communist-supporting workers in Shanghai. The incident is called the April 12 Incident, or the Shanghai Massacre. The 1st United Front between the Nationalists and Communist ends, and the Civil War lasting until 1949 begins.
- April 14 – The first Volvo automobile rolled off the production line in Gothenburg, Sweden.
- April 18 – The Kuomintang (Nationalist Chinese) set up a government in Nanking, China.
- April 21 – A banking crisis hits Japan.
- April 22–May 5 – The Great Mississippi Flood of 1927 strikes 700,000 people in the greatest natural disaster in American history through that time.
- April 27
  - The Carabineros de Chile (Chilean national police force and gendarmery) are created.
  - João Ribeiro de Barros becomes the first non-European to make a transatlantic flight, flying from Genoa, Italy, to Fernando de Noronha, Brazil.

May

- May – Philo Farnsworth of the United States transmits his first experimental electronic TV motion pictures, as opposed to the electromechanical TV systems that others had used before.
- May 9 – The Australian Parliament convenes for the first time in Canberra, Australian Capital Territory. Previously, the Parliament had met in Melbourne, State of Victoria.
- May 11 – The *Academy of Motion Picture Arts and Sciences*, the "Academy" in "Academy Awards", is founded.
- May 12 – British police officers raid the office of the Soviet trade delegation in London.
- May 13 – King George V proclaims the change of his title from King of the United Kingdom of Great Britain and Ireland to King of Great Britain and Northern Ireland.
- May 17 – U.S. Army aviation pioneer Major Harold Geiger dies in the crash of his Airco DH.4 airplane, at Olmsted Field, Pennsylvania.
- May 18 – Bath School disaster: a series of violent attacks results in 45 deaths, mostly of school children, in Bath Township, Michigan.
- May 20 – By the Treaty of Jeddah, the United Kingdom recognizes the sovereignty of Ibn Saud over the Kingdom of Hejaz and Nejd, the future Saudi Arabia.
- May 20–21 – Charles Lindbergh makes the first solo, nonstop transatlantic airplane flight, carried out from New York City to Paris, France, in his single-engined aircraft, the *Spirit of St. Louis*.
- May 22 – A magnitude 8.6 earthquake in Xining, China kills about 200,000 people.
- May 23 – Nearly 600 members of the American Institute of Electrical Engineers and the Institute of Radio Engineers view a live demonstration of television at the Bell Telephone Building in New York City, just over a year after John Logie Baird of Scotland had first demonstrated an *electromechanical television system* to the members of the Royal Society in London.

- May 24 – The United Kingdom cuts its diplomatic relations with the Soviet Union due to revelations of espionage and underground agitation.

May 20: Solo flight New York to Paris

June

- June 4 – Yugoslavia severs diplomatic relations with Albania.
- June 4–6 – Clarence Chamberlin and Charles Albert Levine take off from Roosevelt Field, New York, and fly to Eisleben, Germany, in the Wright-Bellanca WB-2 Columbia aircraft *Miss Columbia*, two weeks after Charles Lindbergh's historic solo flight.
- June 7 – Pyotr Voykov, the Soviet ambassador to Poland, is murdered.
- June 9 – The Soviet Union executes 20 for alleged espionage.
- June 13
    - Léon Daudet, the leader of the French monarchists, is arrested in France.
    - A ticker tape parade is held for the aviator Charles Lindbergh down 5th Avenue in New York City.
- June 28 – *Iberia* Spanish Airlines is established.
- June 29 – A total eclipse of the sun takes place over Wales, northern England, southern Scotland, Norway, northern Sweden, northmost Finland, and the northmost extremes of Russia.
- June 29-July 1 – Commander Richard E. Byrd, Bernt Balchen, George Noville, and Bert Acosta take off from Roosevelt Field, New York, in the Fokker Trimotor airplane *America* and cross the Atlantic to the coast of France, having to ditch there because of bad weather. All four men survive the emergency landing.

July

- July 1 – The Food, Drug, and Insecticide Administration (FDIA) is established as a United States federal agency.
- July 10 – Kevin O'Higgins, Vice-President of the Executive Council of the Irish Free State and Minister for Justice, is assassinated by the anti-Treaty Irish Republican Army in Dublin.
- July 11 – The 1927 Jericho earthquake strikes Palestine, killing around 300 people. The effects are especially severe in Nablus, but damage and fatalities are also reported in many areas of Palestine and Transjordan such as Amman, Salt, Jordan, and Lydda.
- July 13 (Wednesday, Tamuz 13, 5687): 12:30 – Rebbe Yosef Yitzchak Schneersohn is freed from the imprisonment which began on June 15 (Wednesday, Sivan 15, 5687) at 02:15 in exile in the Russian town of Kostroma.
- July 15 – July Revolt of 1927: 85 protesters and five policemen are left dead after the police in Vienna fire on an angry crowd, mostly members of the Social Democratic Party of Austria; more than 600 people are injured.
- July 24 – The Menin Gate is dedicated as a war memorial at Ypres, Belgium.

August

- August 1 – The Communist Chinese People's Liberation Army is formed during the Nanchang Uprising.
- August 2 – U.S. President Calvin Coolidge announces, "I do not choose to run for president in 1928."
- August 7 – The Peace Bridge opens between Fort Erie, Ontario and Buffalo, New York.
- August 10 – The Mount Rushmore Park is rededicated. President Calvin Coolidge promises national funding for the proposed carving of the presidential figures.

- August 22 – 200 people demonstrate in Hyde Park, London against the death sentencing of Italian immigrant anarchists Sacco and Vanzetti.
- August 23 – Sacco and Vanzetti are executed.
- August 24 – August 25 – Hurricane hits the Atlantic Provinces of Canada, causing massive damage and at least 56 deaths.
- August 26 – Paul R. Redfern leaves Brunswick, Georgia, flying his Stinson Detroiter "Port of Brunswick" to attempt a solo nonstop flight to Rio de Janeiro, Brazil. He later crashes in the Venezuelan jungle, but the crash site has never been found.

September

- September – The Autumn Harvest Uprising occurs in China.
- September 7 – The University of Minas Gerais is founded in Brazil.
- September 18 – The Columbia Phonographic Broadcasting System (later known as *CBS*) is formed and goes on the air with 47 radio stations.
- September 25 – A treaty signed by the League of Nations Slavery Commission abolishes all types of slavery.
- September 27 – 79 are killed and 550 are injured in the East St. Louis Tornado, the 2nd costliest and at least 24th deadliest tornado in U.S. history.

October

- October – The Fifth Solvay Conference, held in the latter half of the month, establishes the acceptance of the Copenhagen interpretation.
- October 4 – The actual carving begins at Mount Rushmore, South Dakota.
- October 6 – *The Jazz Singer* opens in the United States and it becomes a huge success, although silent films continue to be made for some time.

- October 8 – *Murderers' Row*: The New York Yankees complete a four-game sweep of the Pittsburgh Pirates in the World Series.
- October 9 – The Mexican government crushes a rebellion in Veracruz.
- October 18 – The first flight of Pan American Airways takes off from Key West, Florida, bound for Havana, Cuba.
- October 25 – The Italian steamer ship *Principessa Mafalda* capsizes off Porto Seguro, Brazil. At least 314 people are killed.
- October 27
  - Queen Wilhelmina of the Netherlands opens the Meuse-Waal Canal in Nijmegen, Holland
  - At 5:50 a.m. a ground fault gives way, causing the mine and part of the town of Worthington to collapse into a large chasm located in Ontario. Nobody is injured in the incident, as the area had been evacuated the night before after a mine foreman noticed abnormal rock shifts in the mine.

November

- November 1 – İsmet İnönü forms a new government in Turkey (The 5th government).
- November 3 – November 4 – Floods devastating Vermont cause the "worst natural disaster in the state's history".
- November 4 – Frank Heath and his horse *Gypsy Queen* return to Washington, D.C., having completed a two-year journey of 11,356 miles to all 48 of the states (of that time).
- November 12
  - Mahatma Gandhi makes his first and last visit to Ceylon.
  - Leon Trotsky is expelled from the Soviet Communist Party, leaving Joseph Stalin with undisputed control of the Soviet Union.
  - The Holland Tunnel opens to traffic as the first vehicular tunnel under the Hudson River linking New Jersey with New York City.
- November 14 – The Pittsburgh gasometer explosion: Three *Equitable Gas* storage tanks in the North Side of Pittsburgh

explode, killing 26 people and causing damage estimated between $4.0 million and $5.0 million.

- November 21 – The Colorado state police open fire on 500 rowdy but unarmed miners during a strike, killing six of them.

December

- December – The Communist Party Congress condemns all *deviation from the general party line* in the USSR.
- December 2 – Following 19 years of Ford Model T production, the Ford Motor Company unveils the Ford Model A as its new automobile.
- December 14 – Iraq gains independence from the United Kingdom.
- December 15 – Marion Parker, 12, is kidnapped in Los Angeles. Her dismembered body is found on December 19, prompting the largest manhunt to date on the West Coast for her killer, William Edward Hickman, who is arrested on December 22 in Oregon.
- December 17 – The United States Navy submarine *S-4* is accidentally rammed and sunk by the United States Coast Guard cutter *John Paulding* off Provincetown, Massachusetts, killing everyone aboard despite several unsuccessful attempts to raise the submarine.
- December 19 –3 Indian Revolutionaries, viz Pandit Ram Prasad Bismil, Thakur Roshan Singh, and Ashfaqulla Khan, are executed by the British Raj. Rajendra Nath Lahiri had been executed two days before.
- December 27 – Kern and Hammerstein's musical play, *Show Boat*, based on Edna Ferber's novel, opens on Broadway and then goes on to become the first great classic of the American musical theater.
- December 30 – The first Japanese commuter metro line, the Tokyo Metro Ginza Line, opens.

Date unknown

- The British Broadcasting Corporation is granted a Royal Charter of Incorporation.
- Harold Stephen Black invents the feedback amplifier.
- The Voluntary Committee of Lawyers is founded to bring about the Repeal of Prohibition in the United States.
- World population reaches two billion.
- In Britain, 1,000 people a week die from an influenza epidemic.

Births

January

Barbara Rush

Olof Palme

- January 1
    - Vernon L. Smith, American economist, Nobel Prize laureate
    - Doak Walker, American football player (d. 1998)
- January 4 – Barbara Rush, American actress
- January 5 – Satguru Sivaya Subramuniyaswami, American-born Hindu guru (d. 2001)

- January 10
  - Gisele MacKenzie, Canadian-born singer (d. 2003)
  - Johnnie Ray, American singer (d. 1990)
  - Otto Stich, member of the Swiss Federal Council (d. 2012)
- January 13
  - Brock Adams, American politician (d. 2004)
  - Sydney Brenner, South African biologist, Nobel Prize laureate
- January 17
  - Thomas Anthony Dooley III, American physician and humanitarian (d. 1961)
  - Eartha Kitt, African-American actress and singer (d. 2008)
- January 23 – Jack Quinlan, Chicago Cubs Radio Broadcaster (d. 1965)
- January 24 – Lasse Pöysti, Finnish writer and playwright
- January 25
  - Antônio Carlos Jobim, Brazilian composer (d. 1994)
  - Gregg Palmer, American actor (d. 2015)
- January 26 – José Azcona del Hoyo, President of Honduras (d. 2005)
- January 28
  - Per Oscarsson, Swedish actor (d. 2010)
  - Hiroshi Teshigahara, Japanese director (d. 2001)
- January 29
  - Edward Abbey, American environmentalist (d. 1989)
  - Don Morrow, American actor and announcer
  - Lewis Urry, Canadian inventor (d. 2004)
- January 30
  - Olof Palme, Prime Minister of Sweden (d. 1986)
  - Bendapudi Venkata Satyanarayana, Indian dermatologist (d. 2005)

February

Sidney Poitier

- February 1 – Galway Kinnell, American poet (d. 2014)
- February 2
  - Stan Getz, American musician (d. 1991)
  - Doris Sams, American female professional baseball player (d. 2012)
- February 3
  - Val Doonican, Irish singer and entertainer (d. 2015)
  - Blas Ople, Filipino politician (d. 2003)
- February 7
  - Juliette Gréco, French singer and actress
  - Vladimir Kuts, Russian runner (d. 1975)
- February 10 – Leontyne Price, African-American soprano
- February 11 – Nalda Bird, American female professional baseball player (d. 2004)
- February 12 – Rita Meyer, American female professional baseball player (d. 1992)
- February 14
  - Seizō Katō, Japanese voice actor (d. 2014)
  - Lois Maxwell, Canadian actress (d. 2007)
- February 15 – Harvey Korman, American actor and comedian (d. 2008)
- February 16 – June Brown, British actress
- February 17 – John Selfridge, American mathematician (d. 2010)
- February 20
  - Roy Cohn, American lawyer and anti-Communist (d. 1986)

- o Sidney Poitier, African-American actor
- February 21
  - o Erma Bombeck, American writer and humorist (d. 1996)
  - o Hubert de Givenchy, French fashion designer
- February 23
  - o Régine Crespin, French operatic soprano (d. 2007)
  - o Ivan Hrušovský, Slovak composer (d. 2001)
  - o Mirtha Legrand, Argentinian actress and TV presenter
- February 24
  - o Mark Lane, American conspiracy theorist (d. 2016)
  - o Emmanuelle Riva, French actress
- February 25 – Ralph Stanley, American bluegrass artist
- February 26 – Tom Kennedy, American game show host
- February 27 – Lynn Cartwright, American actress (d. 2004)

March

Gabriel García Márquez

- March 1
  - o Harry Belafonte, African-American musician and actor
  - o Robert Bork, American conservative law professor (d. 2012)
- March 3 – Pierre Aubert, member of the Swiss Federal Council (d. 2016)
- March 4
  - o Philip Batt, 29th Governor of the U.S. state of Idaho
  - o Thayer David, American actor (d. 1978)
  - o Robert Orben, American magician
  - o Dick Savitt, American tennis player
  - o

- March 6
  - William J. Bell, American soap creator (d. 2005)
  - Gordon Cooper, American astronaut (d. 2004)
  - Gabriel García Márquez, Colombian author, Nobel Prize laureate (d. 2014)
- March 8
  - Dick Hyman, American composer and pianist
- March 10
  - Jupp Derwall, German football player and manager (d. 2007)
  - Marlia Hardi, Indonesian actress (d. 1984)
- March 11
  - Ron Todd, British trade union leader (d. 2005)
  - Joachim Fuchsberger, German-Australian actor, television host, lyricist and businessman (d. 2014)
- March 12 – Raúl Ricardo Alfonsín, former President of Argentina (d. 2009)
- March 13 – Robert Denning, American interior designer (d. 2005)
- March 15
  - Annastasia Batikis, Greek-American female professional baseball player
  - Hanns-Joachim Friedrichs, German journalist (d. 1995)
- March 16
  - Vladimir Komarov, Russian cosmonaut (d. 1967)
  - Daniel Patrick Moynihan, U.S. Senator from New York (d. 2003)
- March 17 – Roberto Suazo Córdova, President of Honduras
- March 18 – George Plimpton, American writer and actor (d. 2003)
- March 20
  - John Joubert, South African–born British composer
  - Earlene Risinger, American professional baseball player (d. 2008)
- March 21 – Hans-Dietrich Genscher, German politician (d. 2016)
- March 23 – Mato Damjanović, Croatian chess grandmaster (d. 2011)
- March 24 – Martin Walser, German author
- March 25
  - Bill Barilko, Canadian hockey player (d. 1951)

- ○ Monique van Vooren, Belgian-American actress
- March 27
  - ○ Mstislav Rostropovich, Russian cellist and conductor (d. 2007)
  - ○ Barbara Marx Sinatra, American businesswoman and socialite
- March 29 – John Robert Vane, British pharmacologist, Nobel Prize laureate (d. 2004)
- March 31
  - ○ César Chávez, American labor activist, United Farm Workers founder (d. 1993)
  - ○ William Daniels, American actor

April

Ferenc Puskás

Éva Székely

Pope Benedict XVI

Margot Honecker

- April 1 – Peter Cundall, Australian horticulturist and television presenter
- April 2
  - Rita Gam, American actress (d. 2016)
  - Ferenc Puskás, Hungarian footballer (d. 2006)
  - Kenneth Tynan, English theatre critic (d. 1980)
- April 3 – Éva Székely, Hungarian swimmer
- April 5 – Chao-Li Chi, Shanxi-born actor (d. 2010)
- April 6 – Gerry Mulligan, American musician (d. 1996)
- April 8 – Tilly Armstrong (alias Tania Langley and Kate Alexander), British writer (d. 2010)
- April 10 – Marshall Warren Nirenberg, American scientist, Nobel Prize laureate (d. 2010)
- April 14 – Alan MacDiarmid, New Zealand chemist, Nobel Prize laureate (d. 2007)
- April 15 – Robert Mills, American physicist (d. 1999)
- April 16
  - Pope Benedict XVI
  - Peter Mark Richman, American actor
- April 17 – Margot Honecker, East German politician (d. 2016)

- April 18
  - Samuel P. Huntington, American political scientist (d. 2008)
  - Charles Pasqua, French businessman and politician (d. 2015)
- April 20
  - Phil Hill, American race car driver (d. 2008)
  - Karl Alexander Müller, Swiss physicist, Nobel Prize laureate
- April 26
  - Anita Darian, American singer and actress (d. 2015)
  - Harry Gallatin, American basketballer and coach (d. 2015)
- April 27 – Coretta Scott King, African-American civil rights leader, wife of Dr. Martin Luther King Jr. (d. 2006)
- April 29 – Lois Florreich, American female professional baseball player (d. 1991)

May

- May 5 – Pat Carroll (actress), American actress
- May 9 – Manfred Eigen, German biophysicist, recipient of the Nobel Prize in Chemistry
- May 9 – Wim Thoelke, German television entertainer (d. 1995)
- May 11
  - Bernard Fox, English actor (*Bewitched*)
  - Mort Sahl, Canadian-born comedian, political commentator
  - Gene Savoy, American author, explorer, scholar and cleric (d. 2009)
- May 13 – Herbert Ross, American film director (d. 2001)
- May 20 – Bud Grant, Canadian and American football coach
- May 22 – George Andrew Olah, Hungarian-born chemist, Nobel Prize laureate
- May 23 – Dieter Hildebrandt, German comedian (d. 2013)
- May 25 – Robert Ludlum, American author (d. 2001)
- May 26 – Endel Tulving, Estonian-Canadian experimental psychologist and cognitive neuroscientist
- May 28 – Ralph Carmichael, American composer and arranger
- May 30
  - Clint Walker, American actor
  - Elly Stone, American singer

June

Jerry Stiller

- June 3 – Boots Randolph, American saxophone player (d. 2007)
- June 4 - Geoffrey Palmer (actor), British actor As Time Goes By (TV series)
- June 8 – Jerry Stiller, American comedian and actor
- June 10 – Ladislao Kubala, Hungarian football player and manager (d. 2002)
- June 12 – Al Fairweather, Scottish jazz musician (d. 1993)
- June 18 – Paul Eddington, British actor (d. 1995)
- June 20 – Bernard Cahier, French F1 photo journalist (d. 2008)
- June 21 – Carl Stokes, American politician (d. 1996)
- June 23 – Bob Fosse, American choreographer and director (d. 1987)
- June 24 – Martin Lewis Perl, American physicist, Nobel Prize laureate (d. 2014)
- June 25 – Chuck Smith, American pastor (d. 2013)
- June 27
  - Bob Keeshan, American actor and children's television show host (d. 2004)
  - Bobby Myers, American NASCAR driver (d. 1957)
- June 28 – Frank Sherwood Rowland, American chemist, Nobel Prize laureate (d. 2012)

July

Gina Lollobrigida

- July 4
  - Gina Lollobrigida, Italian actress
  - Neil Simon, American playwright
- July 6
  - Alan Freeman, Australian-born broadcaster and disc jockey (d. 2006)
  - Janet Leigh, American actress (d. 2004)
  - Pat Paulsen, American comedian and political satirist (d. 1997)
- July 7 -- Doc Severinsen American musician Johnny Carson Show
- July 9 – David Diop, French West African poet (d. 1960)
- July 10
  - David Dinkins, African-American Mayor of New York City from 1989 through 1993
  - William Smithers, American actor
- July 15 – Joe Turkel, American actor
- July 17 – Roy Stuart, American actor (d. 2005)
- July 18 – Kurt Masur, Silesian-born conductor (d. 2015)
- July 26 – Danny La Rue, Irish drag queen (d. 2009)
- July 28 -- John Ashbery, Poet
- July 30 – Victor Wong, American actor (d. 2001)

August

- August 4 – Jess Thomas, American tenor (d. 1993)
- August 7

- o Edwin W. Edwards, American politician
- o Carl Switzer, American actor (d. 1959)
- August 8 – Johnny Temple, American baseball player (d. 1994)
- August 9 – Marvin Minsky, American computer scientist, Turing Award winner (Artificial intelligence) (d. 2016)
- August 11 – Stuart Rosenberg, American director (d. 2007)
- August 12 – Porter Wagoner, American country singer (d. 2007)
- August 14 – Roger Carel (Bancharel), French actor
- August 18 – Rosalynn Carter, wife of U.S. President Jimmy Carter
- August 19 – L. Q. Jones, American actor
- August 20 – Peter Oakley, also known as geriatric1927, British vlogger (d. 2014)
- August 25 – Althea Gibson, African-American tennis player (d. 2003)
- August 26 – Ma Jir Bo, Chinese Realism oil painter (d. 1985)
- August 27 – Fouad al-Tikerly, prominent Iraqi novelist and writer (d. 2008)
- August 30
  - o Geoffrey Beene, American fashion designer (d. 2004)
  - o Bill Daily, American comedian and dramatic actor

September

Peter Falk

- September 3 – Br. John Hamman S.M. (d. 2000), close-up magician, inventor, Marianist brother (d. 2000)
- September 7 – Eric Hill, English author and illustrator (d. 2014)
- September 10 – Johnny Keating, Scottish musician and songwriter (d. 2015)
-

- September 11
  - Vernon Corea, Sri Lankan broadcaster (d. 2002)
  - G. David Schine, American businessman (d. 1996)
- September 16
  - Peter Falk, American actor (d. 2011)
  - Jack Kelly, American actor (d. 1992)
  - Sadako Ogata, Japanese diplomat, former United Nations High Commissioner for Refugees
- September 19
  - Rosemary Harris, American actress
  - Nick Massi, Former Bassist for 'The Four Seasons' (d. 2000)
- September 21
  - Owen Aspinall, 45th Governor of American Samoa (d. 1997)
  - Joan Hotchkis, American actress, writer and performance artist
- September 22
  - Gordon Astall, English footballer
  - Tommy Lasorda, American baseball manager (Los Angeles Dodgers)
- September 24 – Arthur Malet, English actor (d. 2013)
- September 25 – Sir Colin Davis, English conductor (d. 2013)
- September 27 – Steve Stavro, Canadian businessman and sports team owner (d. 2006)
- September 29 – Adhemar Ferreira da Silva, Brazilian athlete (d. 2001)
- September 30 – W. S. Merwin, American poet

October

Roger Moore

Günter Grass

- October 1 – Tom Bosley, American actor (d. 2010)
- October 6 – Antony Grey, English gay rights activist (d. 2010)
- October 8 – César Milstein, Argentine scientist; received the Nobel Prize in Physiology or Medicine (d. 2002)
- October 10 – Dana Elcar, American actor and director (d. 2005)
- October 11 – Princess Joséphine Charlotte of Belgium, Grand Duchess of Luxembourg (d. 2005)
- October 13 – Lee Konitz, American jazz composer and alto saxophonist
- October 14 – Roger Moore, English actor
- October 16 – Günter Grass, German writer, Nobel Prize laureate (d. 2015)
- October 18 – George C. Scott, American actor (d. 1999)
- October 19 – Pierre Alechinsky, Belgian painter
- October 23 – Leszek Kołakowski, Polish philosopher (d. 2009)
- October 24 – Cal Hogue, American baseball player (d 2005)
- October 28 – Roza Makagonova, Russian actress (d. 1995)

November

- November 2 – Steve Ditko, American comic-book writer and artist
- November 3 – Peggy McCay, American actress
- November 5 – Kenneth Waller, English actor (d. 2000)
- November 7 – Hiroshi Yamauchi, Japanese businessman and president of Nintendo (d. 2013)
- November 8 – Patti Page, American singer (d. 2013)
- November 10 – Sabah, Lebanese singer and actress (d. 2014)

- November 14 – McLean Stevenson, American actor (d. 1996)
- November 15 – Gregor Mackenzie, British politician (d. 1992)
- November 17
  - Fenella Fielding, English actress
  - Nicholas Taylor, Geologist, businessman and politician and former Canadian Senator
- November 18 – Hank Ballard, American musician (d. 2003)
- November 21 – Georgia Frontiere, co-owner of the Los Angeles/St. Louis Rams (d. 2008)
- November 23 – Guy Davenport, American author, artist, and scholar (d. 2005)
- November 24
  - Ahmadou Kourouma, Ivorian writer (d. 2003)
  - Alfredo Kraus, Spanish tenor (d. 1999)
- November 28 – Chuck Mitchell, American actor (d. 1992)
- November 29 – Vin Scully, American baseball broadcaster
- November 30 – Robert Guillaume, American actor

December

Bhumibol Adulyadej

Kim Young-sam

- December 2 – Prabhakar Thokal, Indian cartoonist (d. 1999)
- December 3 – Andy Williams, American singer (d. 2012)

- December 5
  - HMK Bhumibol Adulyadej, King of Thailand
  - W. D. Amaradeva, Sri Lanka maestro
  - Óscar Míguez, Uruguayan football player (d. 2006)
  - Erich Probst, Austrian football player (d. 1988)
- December 7 – Helen Watts, Welsh contralto (d. 2009)
- December 8 – Vladimir Shatalov, Russian cosmonaut
- December 9 – Pierre Henry, French composer
- December 12 – Robert Noyce, Intel cofounder (d. 1990)
- December 13 – James Wright, American poet (d. 1980)
- December 17 – Richard Long, American actor (d. 1974)
- December 18 – Roméo LeBlanc, 25th Governor General of Canada (d. 2009)
- December 20
  - Charlie Callas, American comedian and singer (d. 2011)
  - Kim Young-sam, South Korean president (d. 2015)
- December 24 – Mary Higgins Clark, American novelist
- December 25
  - Nellie Fox, American baseball player (d. 1975)
  - Ram Narayan, Indian sarangi player
- December 26
  - Akihiko Hirata, Japanese actor (d. 1984)
  - Alan King, American comedian (d. 2004)
  - Denis Quilley, British actor (d. 2003)
- December 27 – Genevieve Audrey Wagner, American professional baseball player and Doctor of Medicine (d. 1984)
- December 29 – Andy Stanfield, American athlete (d. 1985)
- December 30 – Jan Kubíček, Czech constructivist painter and sculptor (d. 2013)

Deaths

January

- January 9 – Houston Stewart Chamberlain, English-German author (b. 1855)
- January 19 – Empress Carlota of Mexico (b. 1840)

- January 21 – Charles Warren, British police officer and archeologist (b. 1840)

February

- February 4 – Janko Vukotić, Montenegrin general (b. 1866)
- February 13 – Brooks Adams, American historian (b. 1848)
- February 16 – Carl Theodore Vogelgesang, American admiral (b. 1869)
- February 19
  - Fernand de Langle de Cary, French general (b. 1849)
  - Robert Fuchs, Austrian composer (b. 1847)
- February 26
  - Austin M. Knight, American admiral (b. 1854)
  - Hermann Obrist, German sculptor (b. 1862)

March

-
  - March 4
  - Ira Remsen, American chemist, discoverer of saccharin (b. 1846)
  - Max Théon, Polish Jewish occultist (b. 1848)
- March 11 – Xenophon Stratigos, Greek general (b. 1869)
- March 14 – Jānis Čakste, Latvian politician, first president of Latvian Republic (b. 1859)
- March 17 – Charles Emmett Mack, American actor (b. 1900)
- March 22 – Templin Potts, American naval officer; 11th Naval Governor of Guam (b. 1855)
- March 23 – Paul César Helleu, French artist (b. 1859)
- March 25 – Marie-Alphonsine Danil Ghattas, Palestinian Catholic nun, canonized (b. 1843)
- March 27 – Joe Start, American baseball player (b. 1842)

April

- April 15 – Gaston Leroux, French journalist and author (b. 1868)
- April 20 – Enrique Simonet, Spanish painter (b. 1866)

- April 25 – Earle Williams, American actor (b. 1880)

May

- May 2 – Ernest Starling, English physiologist (b. 1866)
- May 3 – Ernest Ball, American singer and songwriter (b. 1878)
- May 8 – Charles Nungesser, French aviator and World War I fighter ace (date of disappearance) (b. 1892)
- May 11 – Juan Gris, Spanish sculptor and painter (b. 1887)

June

- June 1
    - Lizzie Borden, American accused murderer; acquitted of killing her father and stepmother (b. 1860)
    - J. B. Bury, Irish historian (b. 1861)
- June 4 – Robert McKim, American actor (b. 1886)
- June 9 – Victoria Woodhull, American feminist and spiritualist (b. 1838)
- June 11 – William Attewell, English cricketer (b. 1861)
- June 14 – Jerome K. Jerome, English writer (b. 1859)

July

Albrecht Kossel

- July 5
    - Marcelino Crisologo, Filipino politician, playwright, writer and poet (b. 1844)
    - Albrecht Kossel, German physician, recipient of the Nobel Prize in Physiology or Medicine (b. 1853)

- July 8 – Max Hoffmann, German general (b. 1869)
- July 9 – John Drew, Jr., American stage actor (b. 1853)
- July 20 – King Ferdinand of Romania (b. 1865)
- July 24 – Ryūnosuke Akutagawa, Japanese poet and writer (b. 1892)
- July 26 – June Mathis, American screenwriter (b. 1889)

August

- August 13 – James Oliver Curwood, American novelist and conservationist (b. 1878)
- August 17 – Johannes Theodor Baargeld, German painter and poet (b. 1892)
- August 23
  - Nicola Sacco, Italian anarchist (b. 1891)
  - Bartolomeo Vanzetti, Italian anarchist (b. 1888)
- August 24 – Manuel Díaz Rodríguez, Venezuelan writer (b. 1871)

September

- September 1 – Amelia Bingham, American stage actress (b. 1869)
- September 5
  - Marcus Loew, American theatre chain founder (b. 1870)
  - Wayne Wheeler, American temperance movement leader (b. 1868)
- September 14
  - Hugo Ball, German poet, founder of *Dadaism* (b. 1886)
  - Isadora Duncan, British-based American dancer (b. 1877)
- September 19 – Michael Ancher, Danish painter (b. 1849)

Willem Einthoven

- September 29 – Willem Einthoven, Dutch inventor, recipient of the Nobel Prize in Physiology or Medicine (b. 1860)

October

- October 2 – Svante Arrhenius, Swedish chemist, Nobel Prize laureate (b. 1859)
- October 5 – Sam Warner, Hollywood studio executive (b. 1887)
- October 10 – Gustave Whitehead, German-born aviation pioneer (b. 1874)
- October 16 – David Macpherson, Canadian-born American civil engineer (b. 1854)
- October 22
  - Borisav "Bora" Stanković, Serbian writer (b. 1876)
  - Ross Youngs, American baseball player and MLB Hall of Famer (b. 1897)
- October 27 – Joseph "Squizzy" Taylor, Australian underworld figure (b. 1888)

November

- November 1 – Florence Mills, American cabaret singer (b. 1896)
- November 4
  - Hawthorne C. Gray, record-setting American balloonist (b. 1889)
  - Valli Valli, actress (b. 1882)
- November 11 – Wilhelm Johannsen, Danish botanist, physiologist and geneticist (b. 1857)
- November 18 – Emma Carus, American opera contralto, (b. 1879)
- November 23 – Alfred III, Prince of Windisch-Grätz, former Prime Minister of Austria (b. 1851)

December

- December 17
  - Hubert Harrison, African-American writer, critic, and activist (b. 1883)

- ○ Rajendra Nath Lahiri, Indian Revolutionary, Hindustan Republican Association (b.1901)
- December 18 – Pandit Ram Prasad Bismil, Indian Revolutionary, Hindustan Republican Association (b. 1897
- December 19
  - ○ Ashfaqulla Khan, Indian Revolutionary, Hindustan Republican Association (b. 1900)
  - ○ Thakur Roshan Singh, Indian Revolutionary, Hindustan Republican Association (b. 1892)

Nobel Prizes

- Physics – Arthur Holly Compton, Charles Thomson Rees Wilson
  - Chemistry – Heinrich Otto Wieland
  - Physiology or Medicine – Julius Wagner-Jauregg
    - Literature – Henri Bergson
    - Peace – Ferdinand Buisson, Ludwig Quidde

In the news

The Holland Tunnel under the Hudson River opens on November 13th connecting New York City with Jersey.

Charles Lindbergh flies The Spirit of St. Louis across the Atlantic nonstop and solo.

Earthquake measuring 8.6 on Richter scale strikes Xining, China killing 200,000.

Work begins on Mount Rushmore.

In Britain, a 1000 people a week die from influenza epidemic.

First transatlantic telephone call - New York City to London.

1927 Calendar

January 1927
Sun	Mon	Tue	Wed	Thu	Fri	Sat
						1
2	3	4	5	6	7	8
9	10	11	12	13	14	15
16	17	18	19	20	21	22
23	24	25	26	27	28	29
30	31					

February 1927
Sun	Mon	Tue	Wed	Thu	Fri	Sat
		1	2	3	4	5
6	7	8	9	10	11	12
13	14	15	16	17	18	19
20	21	22	23	24	25	26
27	28					

March 1927
Sun	Mon	Tue	Wed	Thu	Fri	Sat
		1	2	3	4	5
6	7	8	9	10	11	12
13	14	15	16	17	18	19
20	21	22	23	24	25	26
27	28	29	30	31		

April 1927
Sun	Mon	Tue	Wed	Thu	Fri	Sat
					1	2
3	4	5	6	7	8	9
10	11	12	13	14	15	16
17	18	19	20	21	22	23
24	25	26	27	28	29	30

May 1927
Sun	Mon	Tue	Wed	Thu	Fri	Sat
1	2	3	4	5	6	7
8	9	10	11	12	13	14
15	16	17	18	19	20	21
22	23	24	25	26	27	28
29	30	31				

June 1927
Sun	Mon	Tue	Wed	Thu	Fri	Sat
			1	2	3	4
5	6	7	8	9	10	11
12	13	14	15	16	17	18
19	20	21	22	23	24	25
26	27	28	29	30		

July 1927
Sun	Mon	Tue	Wed	Thu	Fri	Sat
					1	2
3	4	5	6	7	8	9
10	11	12	13	14	15	16
17	18	19	20	21	22	23
24	25	26	27	28	29	30
31						

August 1927
Sun	Mon	Tue	Wed	Thu	Fri	Sat
	1	2	3	4	5	6
7	8	9	10	11	12	13
14	15	16	17	18	19	20
21	22	23	24	25	26	27
28	29	30	31			

September 1927
Sun	Mon	Tue	Wed	Thu	Fri	Sat
				1	2	3
4	5	6	7	8	9	10
11	12	13	14	15	16	17
18	19	20	21	22	23	24
25	26	27	28	29	30	

October 1927
Sun	Mon	Tue	Wed	Thu	Fri	Sat
						1
2	3	4	5	6	7	8
9	10	11	12	13	14	15
16	17	18	19	20	21	22
23	24	25	26	27	28	29
30	31					

November 1927
Sun	Mon	Tue	Wed	Thu	Fri	Sat
		1	2	3	4	5
6	7	8	9	10	11	12
13	14	15	16	17	18	19
20	21	22	23	24	25	26
27	28	29	30			

December 1927
Sun	Mon	Tue	Wed	Thu	Fri	Sat
				1	2	3
4	5	6	7	8	9	10
11	12	13	14	15	16	17
18	19	20	21	22	23	24
25	26	27	28	29	30	31

U.K bank Holidays

Saturday, January 1	New Year's Day
Monday, February 14	Valentine's Day
Tuesday, March 1	Shrove Tuesday
Tuesday, March 1	St. David's Day
Wednesday, March 2	Ash Wednesday
Thursday, March 17	St. Patrick's Day
Sunday, March 27	Mothering Sunday
Friday, April 1	April Fool's Day
Thursday, April 14	Maundy Thursday
Friday, April 15	Good Friday
Sunday, April 17	Easter
Saturday, April 23	St. George's Day
Sunday, May 1	May Day
Monday, May 30	Spring Bank Holiday
Tuesday, July 12	Orangemen's Day
Monday, August 29	Late Summer Bank Holiday
Monday, October 31	Halloween
Saturday, November 5	Guy Fawkes Day
Saturday, December 24	Christmas Eve
Sunday, December 25	Christmas
Monday, December 26	Boxing Day
Saturday, December 31	New Year's Eve

Printed in Great Britain
by Amazon